T0328485

NAKED TRUTH

POEMS

Kraftgriots

Also in the series (POETRY)

NAKED TRUTH
POEMS

Chris Anyokwu

kraftgriots

Published by

Kraft Books Limited
6A Polytechnic Road, Sango, Ibadan
Box 22084, University of Ibadan Post Office
Ibadan, Oyo State, Nigeria
✆ + 234 (0)803 348 2474, + 234 (0)805 129 1191
E-mail: kraftbooks@yahoo.com
www.kraftbookslimited.com

First published 2015

ISBN 978-978-918-329-6

= KRAFTGRIOTS =
(A literary imprint of Kraft Books Limited)

First printing, October 2015

Dedication

For

'Gbenga Adegoke

Words, and even tears
Have failed to assuage
The pain of your untimely
And inexplicable passage,
I hope these offerings
Will lessen my sorrow
And stanch my tears.

Selah

Now, for the poet, he nothing affirms, and therefore never lieth. For, as I take it, to lie is to affirm that to be true which is false, so as the other artists, and especially the historian, affirming many things, can, in the cloudy knowledge of mankind, hardly escape from many lies. But the poet (as I said before) never affirmeth. The poet never maketh any circles about your imagination, to conjure you to believe for true what he writes. He citeth not authorities of other histories, but even for his entry calleth the sweet Muses to inspire into him a good invention; in truth, not labouring to tell you what is, or is not, but what should or should not be.

–Sir Philip Sidney, *An Apology for Poetry*

Contents

TRUTH ABOUT HERE AND THERE

Naked truth

They call them a pack of parasites
Feeding off the gurgling ventricles of others
Be it ideas, conceptual categories or the things
They give birth to: from tooth-pick to tractor
Democracy to Neurosis
All on credit they borrow

The nation is a will-o'-the-wisp;
A hunting-dog that went a-missing in the Berlin forest of
divisive cobbling
The hunter and the hound now hunt each other
For the centre which refuses to hold
Divided tongues spew sundering visions
Spawning a cult of mediocrity and ethnicity its kin's vice
Which drag the people down Mungo Park's dissembling
cataract
Divided we stand, for unity is a poisoned chalice
From which their helmsmen flee
Although they mouth the mantra like pious *almajiri*
Constitutional Reform is a lifetime rigmarole
Like Babangida's Transition
That promised to deliver on the dividends of democracy
Before the Second Coming
Waiting, always waiting for the Godot of the good life
Espied in 1960
Before they struck, warred and rose up
To pick the pieces of their ungatherable lives
Soldier go, soldier come
Civilian caretakers surprise the house like timorous mice
Scuttling into hiding at the sound of approaching jackboots
Soldier go, soldier come
It's merely a change of wardrobe, sartorial makeover

Of the circus chameleon, the fop that flunks
Leadership 101 for beginners
And that's the crux of the matter
Their forebears, it was, who sold their subjects
For rum and mirror
For gunpowder and tinsel toys
Their fathers, it was, who rode on the people's back
In those Indirect Rule days
While the white man messed with the black mind
Leaving the forest a desert for false christs
Intent on erecting dynasties in perpetuity
Mongrel culture of apes infected with the Ebola of double
consciousness
Half-children raised in orphanages of bastard ideologies
Lilliputians chewing cud of alien grass
In the comity of nations
Ah, here at home
Under the spreading mango tree
Brother sell brother
For friendship died with Biafra and patriotism with heroes
past
But today it exchanges hands like a dud cheque
Seeking to purchase a future
That flees from you like a shadow.

Celebrating a thief

[Trumpet and drums. Then: song]
O ti se o
Baba ti se o (2ce)
Ohun to n bawa leru
Baba ti se o

Baba nla ole rode roughshod over the people's wish
To State House the other day
First he made his bedchambers
The state's coffers, from where he salts away our money
To his countless accounts, his wives' accounts,
His children's and his concubines' secret tills
The leftovers? He used to construct roads
That do not outcast the tape-cutting fanfare;
His electrification project, like all his other IOUs
Are Greek gifts that impoverish the poor
And today is a public holiday
For *Baba nla ole* is visiting our ghetto
Yesterday a water-tank
Went up the skies and a tanker brought
Us the scarce manna
In blinding flashes of camera lights
Our ruler cut the tape and left
Us of our millennial thirst.

O ti se o
Baba ti se o ....

Change came riding on the back of a civil coup
And swept the debris of an erstwhile god
Into gaol and the opposition went to town,
Taunting:

14

Nebu Nebu Nebu
Nebuchadnezzar nje 'we
Ohun to ba aiye wa je
Lana bii Agbako
Nebuchadnezzar nje 'we (2ce)

Yesterday's man of power
Spoke in a voice of thunder
Behind bars and the earth shook
The prison doors opened, his chains fell off
It's celebration time again:
Tail between their hindquarters
His enemies beat an ungainly retreat
As our behemoth took the centre stage again
And the people danced themselves lame
In the broiling sun
Clad in uniform finery bedecked with the thief's
Triumphant face:
Ah, politics is a love potion the rich
Brew for the poor

Talo sope aani baba
Kai, a ni baba (2ce)
Ojelu nla ni baba wa
Kai a ni baba ....

When "swallow" is religion
(Macherata, Italy)

Far far away from home
From *buka* banter over *ewedu* and *amala*
Pounded yam and *egusi* soup
Isi-ewu and *nkwobi*
You roam cute corners,
Manicured walkways
And complex mosaics of paths
Searching for "swallow"
Ah, *eba* or pounded yam is religion
In retrospect—
Kebabs, soup-kitchens and restaurants
Of a thousand tongues
But none speaks the language of "swallow",
African style.
What to do?
You strike *entente* with roaring hunger,
Make truce with your rebellious stomach
Munching tasteless bread
Downed with bitter coffee.
You wear saccharine smiles
And stave off the raging civil war
Within
Counting the seconds on leaden feet
Before departure.

The beggar

Here you are
In icy heaven
Tricked out in habits of strangers
Bowl in hand, running
After cavalier donors
Lisping an oppressor tongue
That puts your own to sleep
A hitch-hiker paddling all night across the Mediterranean
Whose floor clatters with your kinsmen's hapless bones
And the other day on satellite TV
Your brother was smoked out
From a plane-burrow, a stowaway
Fleeing dubious dignity for slavery
After all, it's better to reign in hell
Than to slave in heaven – first son,
Your allotted patch where primogeniture
Is a loud fart that puts out the wick of truth
Since your sinecure herdsmen
Scour the African desert in visible darkness
In order to lead their flock to the border
The fewer the better
Who owns papa's land?
Who owns papa's land?
Does your sibling who sold his titles
To seek existential reprieve in foreign pastures
Have a foothold in the collective estate?
Behold him now, wiser after the fact
Lost in every sense
The chime of coins on begging bowl is
Music to his starving ears
Yet kith and kin at home
Wait for the storied windfall.

When Africans die

When Africans die
They shall go to heaven
Because they are in hell:
A tear-jerker on white TV
Scarecrows of temperate satieties
Tillers of droughts, land and mind
Bean-pole mass of deprivation inmates
Milling millions from forests to savannahs
In eternal search of the meaning-needle in life's haystack
Road mendicants stranded, some in Europe's dump-sites
Others eking out bone-dry existence in America's morgues,
And veggie fields and construction dungeons.
Sheep without shepherds
Bleating a din to an indifferent world
Tired and sick of aid.
Oh, hell has no fury like Africa
Bereft of bare necessities, robbed and denuded
Of basic dignity
From womb to tomb
All we know is Hell's teeth-gnashing
Over perennial funerals of inchoate dreams
Butchered by power-perverts
Fair is fair, when
Hell's inhabitants die
They go to heaven
When Africans die
They shall go to heaven, yes
Because they are in hell ....

Climate change I

At his backyard he heard the roar of the ocean
Rising up to the Kilimanjaro
And crashing down to the sea-level
Yet, not a fin was stolen from the tilapia, neither did
The toad lose its shoal

The forest dense, forbiddingly dense and impassable
The squirrel, the elephant
The ant and the lion;
Animals, big and small,
All had their day in the sun

Yet, the hunter-gatherer
Never hurt a stone
A boulder he never turned
The sylvan denizens he respectfully
Took for food

Now, his progeny
Steal the sun and slay the forest
Poison the sea and rob the earth
So Nature is fighting back:
The ice is melting
Ocean surges a common occurrence
Strange fires devour the community
And soon, we shall be homeless.

Climate change II

What is climate change?
Is it when Night confronts us
When we hope for Day?
When rain pours non-stop
When the sky is supposed to be as dry as the Sahara?

Indeed, what is climate change?
Is it, in fact, when we prepare for Harmattan
But our crops are washed away by relentless deluge?
Or when the cock does not crow at dawn
But rather hurries us off to bed at mid-day
Because the heavens play tricks with its sense of time?

They say it's when our huts (without fire),
Catch fire, our stream turns boa-constrictor
and swallows the fisherman and his gear
They say it's when August Break fails
And the whole village goes downhill
In one humongous watercress

They say it is when Home becomes Diaspora
And the land of strangers becomes Home:
When the climate changes
Time shall also change, taking our homestead with it.
And then all shall return home.

Homo haram

Let us shrink the sky
To a minuscule canopy
To cause a thousand birds
To clash and fall to the earth
For we must banish space and
Institute a time-warp
To relive primal blunderings of the Beginning ...
Oh, blot out the sun
And poison the rain
So that all may grope
Their benighted route to ruin

Traffic

A
   metallic
      snake
         stretches from Cape to Cairo
               trapped in its belly,
        desperate humanity
          parboiled in mobile
             hells for hours on
     end, motionless
      as they watch their
           fond fantasies
        wilt and die
          with the
              setting sun.

Campus girl

It is that time of year again,
Holiday's over when she's required to register
Courses and attend lectures,
But she's got more important urgencies on her plate

There are fripperies to be bought in Dubai,
Tinsel toys of passion to be purchased in Paris
And brisk business to be done in Abuja Hilton
Where Mr. Senator breaks the law between her eager thighs

Then exams are'round the corner, as assignments and
Tests cascade like frozen pellets of rain:
She breezes onto campus, the prima donna of
Gossip magazines, smelling sweetly like the kept-woman

Of an Arabian Sheik, doling out dough to famished dons
To settle and sort her mounting debts.

Meaning

At cockcrow you nestled beside the waking hearth
Energizing the doing hand
And putting taste in the soup of the day's struggles

You were everywhere
Essential like air:
In the laughter of infants
In the steaming rendezvous of mating-birds
In the tos and fros of the road
From mouth to the anus

Life's worthless without you
And now right in broad daylight
You've packed your things and disappeared:

Town crier, rouse the people;
Sound the gong; let hunters release their hounds
And let everybody scour the nooks and crannies
Of the village for meaning is missing;
We are undone
The hand can no longer find the mouth
The tongue has lost its taste
Food has turned ashes in our mouth
And our festivals a perennial funeral;

Oh, meaning, we shall spare no effort
We shall search the skies, the seas, lands
Home and abroad until we find you
And bring you back to where you belong—
Our life.

Ebola

They say you are worse than HIV/AIDS
That even cancer cannot carry your goatskin bag
To the gathering of *Arun*
Malaria, matriarch of Mama Africa, I hear,
Has long abdicated her perch for you, Ebola!

So, is it really true
What they tell me?
That you want to change our way of life?
That you are the knife
Which saw asunder man and wife;
Mother and child, brother and sister;
Friend and dear friend; and even lovers?

Is love now a crime, Ebola?
Shall we, then, sow animosity and water it
Betimes to gross canopy of iron-curtain islands?

Dreaded monsters have ravaged our land before;
Strange meteorites have come and gone
Plagues of unknown nomenclature
Have come and gone
And so shall you, Ebola
And laughter shall remain
On our conquering lips.

Violation

(For Foley killed in Iraq)

Mother Earth is sated
Her womb violated by freak spawn who
Spill brothers' blood like Cain:
You don the mask
You mouth mad mantra of contrary ideology
That makes your brother, your mother's son,
Your sworn enemy
And with the sword
You slit his throat
A common sallah ram
To propitiate the unknown god
Now the homestead is in ruins
Mourning rends the dawn
As you fast-track Armageddon.

Gunpoint faith

(For the Yazidi)

Was it instant death to be dispensed
By the Ak-47 trained at him
That drove him to cross the line?
Or the promise of Nirvana
Peopled by bevies of virgins
That charmed his famished palate
To blur his primal vision of glory?

Or was it just sheer desperation
To cling on to this side of the grave:
Shorn of cacti in this desert of loss?

What, indeed, is the stuff of faith
Force-fed at the point of a gun?

I love to hate you

Let no one stop me
I have a right to hate
Him whom the gods have blessed
Why should he be the fortunate one
And I, the *Oloriburuku?*

I woke up at crack of dawn
Just like him; dipped in the
Village stream for shoals of gems,
Just like him:
While he came away with bounties,
I returned a basket-case.

I love to hate you,
Olorire: your blessings
Advertise my emptiness
And, what does it matter
If you have not stolen my goats or yams?
Encroached on my turf?
Why should the gods be kind to you
But leave me empty-handed?

Pettiness

Pettiness, thy name is Mr. Lecturer
Whose more illustrious colleague's
Vaulting scrolls crow his own brittle achievements:
Stale diet of regurgitated cud;
Faded and dowdy gown of primeval lore
Loud farts mistaken for cerebral profundities
Vainglorious harlequinade on perfumed corridors
Frequented by starry-eyed belles overawed by shopsoiled cant
Spewed by the narcissistic dunce.
Ah, pettiness, thy name is Mr. Lecturer
Whose hobby-horse is a career in
Pull-Him-Down (PhD).

Little minds

Your brother's mistake is your ministry;
You keep eternal ledger of his wrongs;
Keeping vigil for that perfect time
To spill the bean and send him to Golgotha.
Apt-pupil of Mrs. Sparsit:
You construct in your puny mind
Haman's gallows on which your brother, your sworn foe,
Does *gangolova*, see-sawing on your lofty scales
Falling, falling down, down, down ...
Into the morass of your willed perdition.
Pray, Brother, is life itself worth this self-destruct?
Is live-and-let-live a mere fancy buzz-phrase to your sadistic
soul?
Must you abdicate your public life
To pursue a sleuth's shadowy sway?
But remember Haman
For you may wish all you wish
God holds the gavel.

.

Rain maker

Grey-haired Brahmin
Sequestered in a solitary corner
Of the ancient hearth
Dead panned face, a cryptic smile
Playing around the rheumy eyes
He's said to hold court with the heavens
To decree the courses of Nature:
"Let there be no rain"
He tells the cumulus coming to term
For a dearly departed must be committed to earth without rain.
Calling his bluff, the rain;
Heaven came down all night
And our sleep was sweet.

The word (I)

Audible sounds
Uttered through human mouth
To the listening ear
Of matter: fellow man, plant or beast
Or even inanimate objects
And the world is changed
Forever.

Life and death of Rufus

In life:
Who born dis bastard
Wey dey tief people property
Carry anoda man wife
And dey spoil oda people pickin?

Which village im for come sef?
Chai! E no dey obey the law
At all at all
Fear no dey im eye
Anytin wey im wan'do
E go do am, sam-sam

In short im bi Mr. Lawless
Call police for am, *uhmm!*
Call soldier for am, *uhmm!!*
Carry im name go babalawo
Im bi like chameleon wey nobody fit chop!
Rufus, na wa for you …

In death:

Ah, na so life bi
Rufus of all people:
Everybody love am
Im too kind, e bi like God sef!
E dey pay school-fees for oda people pikin
If your wife sick sef
E go carry am for im motor
Go hospital, even people wey no get work
E dey dash dem money.

Common fly, e no dey hurt
I never see any person
Wey good like am
Ah, Rufus, we go miss you ....

Oligie-Igbanke

They say you are the centre-court of flesh-birds
An abbatoir of green shoots
Who early venture to reach the sun
Like a wicked mother you build
Your fireplace with the heads of your children
Surprised that daily your roads narrow
with rank weeds?
That your playgrounds, kneaded in former times,
by busy feet of thronged youth,
are now nurseries of jeering reptiles?
Light bearers, come and go
Their torches drenched by unseasonal downpours
And the darkness thickens
In droves your futures drift,
Drift towards Sodom, jinxed by mirages of alien miracles
Yet at twilight, your spawn, bruised, broken and battered,
return bearing ash.

Betrayal

What is the price of blood
My blood which gave you life
Whilst you grappled with the slippery reins?

A trip or two to the *buka*;
The odd change dropped in lean seasons
Or the benefit of your rowdy company?

I was Man Friday in your moment of power
We both held the levers then,
or so it seemed,

And it made me few friends and a million enemies
And they waited, friends and foes, alike
For us to dismount our power-steed

To settle accounts.
Now, you have moved on to higher ground
And all I get are shots of incubated poison.

What, indeed, is the price of my blood?
A knife in the back?

The politician's paradise

The Baale: Government, we the people thank you
For remembering us and for choosing
To visit our ghetto in spite of all of these:
Our impassable streets and roads; and lack
of electricity.
Our gutters full of flotsam and jetsam.
In fact, we cleared our children's playground
For your helicopter; and see how our people,
old and
Young are salivating at the flying bird!
All we ask, Government, is a little dignity
To live and die with. Then you shall have our
votes.

The Politician: My people, I feel your pain
Your suffering is my suffering
Remember I am one of you:
Roofless and shoeless. Once.
But I promise you, my people,
I shall remove the sun
And give you heaven on earth
Paved with a million suns and stars.
I shall turn your ghetto into GRA
Your children shall be driven to school in
limos
And you all shall live and never die.
Just vote me into power
And I shall give you paradise.

Chimamanda

Feline wrestler whose back and the ground
Are sworn enemies; for her exploits
Are gifts from the eternal Guardians of the cosmos

If you seek or search for them
Look no farther than their messenger
Racing from the tropics to icy climes

With blazons of good tidings
The word is her wand
Deployed in leading the way to Prometheus' fire

Ask Achebe, the *alusi* of sage sooth
He will tell you his daughter came down
The celestial rafters, almost fully made.
Ask Beyonce who *knows* the wordsworth
In the fight of their kind.

Ah, happy feminist:
You've sat at the feet of worthy Amazons
And patriarchs of the Word alike
You now reign, master of nuance and nous
As you dispense light to a groping world.

Keep your job

When men play God:
They send a child for salt
And unleash rain as escort
They give you fire to bear on naked palm
Lashed left, right and centre
With trade hazards and bait your
Patched palate with nectars
Even the gods will gulp in a swig
And then plant IEDs and booby-traps
For your longing pike
And wait, like king cobra,
For the venom to lead you to hell.
Oh, ye small men playing God
Keep your job
For He who sates the sparrow
My account has settled.

Earth

Mother Earth
Here the items for the sacrifice:
All the talents, all the money, my certificates and the joys, and
The fame they've brought me
And, above all, here is the final sacrifice—Me.

There's a whole lot of people going home
Carrying with them absolutely nothing
Having smashed and grabbed
Toiled and tilled
Milking your bounteous udders
Which sustain the stock

Yes, Mother, yours is the unstinting openhandedness of a
Loving benefactor: see the child bounding about,
Fancy-free; the youth sating the heady opiate of summer;
And age pilgrimming gracefully to the waiting sea ...

Mother Earth, patience is your name
For when our race is run in scrambled time
All return to your womb
Void, for the endless whirligig.

Grace

Bottomless pouch into which the undeserving dip
To collect cowries to defray life's sundry debts
It laughs at the Law's iron sway
And shatters the prison door to set prisoners free
It's a miracle of freedom
From all life's givens
Last-gasp reprieve to earth's condemned
It's inexhaustible riches for the desperate poor.

Free spirit

Do you spread the net
Before the vigilant bird;
The baited hook in the face of the fish?
Then why tie my peripatetic feet
With chains of custom; unleash thought-police to sleuth my
busy mind,
Imprison my tongue in hushes
Of Thou-Shalt-Nots?
I make my own laws
And break my bounds:
I create my own world
With dappled loam of rich fancies
The earth is my playground
Man and beast obey my command
And all nature kowtows to my caprices
So watch me as I take virgin territories
Annex turfs of novel darings
And reign sovereign wherever I go.

Be yourself
(For Zainab)

Buoyed by arpeggios of deluded prima donnas
And wafted on skeins of uniform nosegays
Purchased with proceeds of violated sanctities
They, all of them, caper about the Ivory stairways
On stilettos of giddy girlhood:
Not for them duels of febrile pursuits
Not for them aureoles of the cerebral holy grail
Nor the exalted rites of intellectual passage
But the hoisting of gilded flags
On the temple of Venus
And the endless orgies of Aphrodite.
Here, it's all show:
The careful cultivation of selves other than yours
A death-in-life the myopic mistake for identity.

Hope

Hope's a dying plant
Which is starved of nutrients
And yet stubbornly clings on to
A stony soil.
Then, next, at
DAWN
Green shoots greet the doubting eye
And suddenly all's well,
Again.

Portrait of a she-don

Reedy, gnarled, gaunt and sour:
Personal epithets she has picked up
In her trough of triumph to her chair
Yet as she daily beholds them, the careless generation,
As she calls them, she returns ...

A long day at the catechist's:
An ordeal of cud-chewing, a ewe
Tethered to the baobab of mores and imported chains;
After a wearying hide-and-seek
Her hide's ruptured by holy rod
A life-time of penance follows and, like gall,
It embitters everything thenceforth:
Schooling, matrimony, religiosity, social work—
All, one ritual of self-immolation and salvation-seeking.
For her, it's all work, not grace, the female Christ
To whom the world is beholden ...

And as she looks at them,
Fancy-free and footloose,
Feckless and carefree, eating their ice-cream
And chewing their gum, necking and carousing,
Roving birds for whom the blue sky remains eternally
Capacious and free,
She's overcome by strange messianism
As she forges in her crowded heart
A million crosses for the careless generation.

Friendship

Faded flower in the "post" — garden
Wilted and trampled under your lover's insensate feet;
Wielding the deafening anvil of the urgent:
In her dictionary the entry
Reads archaic, antiquated, out-of-use;
Yet a magic wand for all seasons
The cat's spur for pulling burning chestnuts out
Of the fire; the timeless blackmail
That gets all jobs done.
She reaches for it post-haste
To clang you awake to her urgencies;
For restoring equilibrium, her peace of mind after threats of storm
Guarantees your brief.

Seasons

Rain or shine, the billows
Neigh bolting skyhigh like refractory horses
Capsizing sundry rafts soughing the waters
For sacrifices for the ever-demanding god:
Early birds and twilight risers
Both same harvest gathering in,
Loss
Strapping youth and sinewy age
Both struggle to gain the shoal
To return to earth, laden with bounties
Yet even the favoured come to shore
With empty dragnets full of gravity-stones.
Hope springs with the dawn
Belying even contrary portents
Blinding the eyes to certain cataracts
But, like vapour, disappears
In the face of bruising suns
Leaving the paddler, floundering into jinxed vortex
At nightfall, he manages to regain shore
For the repeated time.

Charity

Here Charity is homeless
For prejudice has driven
Her out of doors
On the college corridor
You face West and
I face East
We both dismantle
The career ladder that gyres to
The professional skies
At the secretariat
Tongues tear us apart
And there's nowhere to hide
From the ethnicity conflagration
That's ravaging the national shack
In the international conference
Strangers wear a racist scowl
And give you a wide berth
The leper from Heart of Darkness
Would somebody get this black trash
Off my face, please?
Here Charity is homeless
For prejudice has driven
Her out of doors.

Do you want to teach me my job?

A chronic latecomer
With utterly no sense of time
He likes to keep everybody
Waiting
Whilst he fumbles and bungles
Wrestling with blunt tools
Where cutting-edge ideas and sheer
Commonsense are required.
Point this out, and he fires back:
Do you want to teach me my job?

It doesn't matter
What chair
He occupies:
Lawyer or doctor
Nurse or teacher
Secretary or CEO
Policeman or driver
Vulcanizer or *Mama put*
Engineer or farmer
Pastor or Imam
Bricklayer or *Maiguard*.
He wobbles and fumbles at a standstill
While time whizzes by
A supersonic carrier
Of the Next Generation.
Look around you
Report cards of his industry
Stare you in the face:
Prison yards swarming with *ATM**
Emptying wards, over flowing morgues,
A land of cerebral *keregbes***

Uneducatable, unemployable educated illiterates;
It's a nation in permanent *go-slow****
Regressing to primeval superstitions
In the high noon of space shuttle.
Our friend wears a wristwatch
But pays scant attention to
Time and detail.
Suggest this and he fires back:
Do you want to teach me my job?

---

*   *Awaiting Trial Men (ATM)*
**   *dwarfs*
*** *traffic snarl-up*

Memory

The bird wings
Its way from perch to perch
Tufts of food in mouth
To slay hunger for self and brood.
It runs its biological clock
In ordered time or painful end.
End of story, it goes home
Leaving no trace behind.
Like the bird,
Kindred spirit

I
Hustle and bustle
Staking out enclaves, stacking up
Treasures
Children, certificates, estates,
All, testaments of my journey and
Like the bird
Kindred spirit
I run my course
And return, empty-handed
Memory and death haggle over
My name; and death queries:
Memory, what's your span?
And memory replies: eternity.

In my father's house

In my father's house
There are many mansions
Occupied by infant ghosts
Sentries over peace that
Lies shattered like shards
Of mirror
Reflecting our cracks and crevices
That seduce owls at night and
Lizards during the day.

In my father's house
Mother murders her brimming brood
Vaulting young stalks
Searching for sunlight
And precious rain
To water our parched calloused lot.

In my father's house
We eat dinner spiced with hemlock
And at daybreak
The town crier keens our latest loss:
The family eldest, soaring in urban skies, lies
Now cold as ice.

In my father's house
Shadows roam around
With bolts of venom
Reptiles are creepers
That vein the lintel.

In my father's house
Dreams die at dawn.

Life

Crowding the void
With activity
Giving taste to the white
Of an Egg
Routing the silence
Of Non-meaning
To leave behind
The ruins
Slags of memory

You are not my God

Hammocked in delusions
And daring Nature's sway
A tin-god over mortal miseries
Parcelling out destinies
To minions, fawners on
Bloated flatulence of hubris
They grovel at your feet
Of clay, and tug at your tuxedo
Of straw
Your beaded crown,
Flimsy skeins of connections
To power covens, wads stacked away
Here and there and, perhaps
A minor shed that offers shelter
To few forlorn from privation.
Thus rigged up on your flaky throne,
You look down
And see a fly gliding, dreaming,
Walking its talk
Of decent dignity, greatness
Perhaps.
Avoiding poisons of sloth, reaching
Beyond turds of puniness and
Winging its way skywards, the realms
Of satieties, to shame crabs and butterflies.
You lie in wait
Biding your time, to ambush its noble dreams
To swell your catacombs of ill-wish.
But remember, your own life
Is a vapour and tomorrow
Is beyond your twisted gambit

I rise
Regardless
And touch the sky
For you are not my God.

Arsenal

Ever seen a more breath—
Taking romance between foot
And ball; the red-and-white
Dancers caressing the round leather
Among them, the troupe's choreographer,
Arsene Wenger, aquiline tactician
Frenchifying proceedings before
An overawed, hypnotized world?
To a drab, woe-begone world
A feast of beautiful football,
Arsenal-style, makes all the difference.
They may be long on aesthetics and
Short the trophy haul
But what are hollow cymbals
To a somnolent audience?
Give me a turbo-charged
Adrenalin-pumping match
Yes, let's have poetry of the feet
in silky sex with the ball
Thank you very much.
Some do pack the bus
Some are toughies in the wrong calling
Turning the lush down into ogres' lair
For these and company
The end justifies the meanness
Giving the game a bad name.
But no worries, folks
Sit back, relax and let
Arsenal take you to Nirvana.

Alaaru

Alaaru snatches a bit
Of a reprieve in the unforgiving sun
From his endless toing and froing in the belly of the
Skyscraper under construction
In upscale Business District.
And he tries to divert himself
With today's newspaper:
"Senate Approves ₦100 Trillion Budget";
"Federal Govt. Secures $50 Billion Chinese Loan"
"Federal Executive Council okays ₦500 Billion Irrigation
Project"...
Angry and hungry, *Alaaru* skims
Through the pages, break-time coming to an end:
"Quantitative Leasing"...
"Liquidity Flow"...
"New International Airport Planned"...
"IMF Chief Due In The Country Tomorrow"; "World Bank...",
- oh, God!
"GDP Skyrockets and Per Capita Income in All-time High"...
And ... finally,
"Unemployment plummets to 0.01%!!!"
Losing it, *Alaaru* cries:
What's all this grammar
Got to do with the price of *garri*?

[*Alaaru: Yoruba word for a kind of all-purpose labourer*]

Wordplay

Aid
Aids
The aid of AIDs
The AIDs of aid
Aid
Aids.

African studies

They sit in heaven
And occupy Moses' seat
And periscope Egypt's welts and woes
Through prisms of doctored history
Willed wastelands of distant satellites
Slaves of yore
Mendicants of today and
Ghosts of tomorrow.
A people without tongue,
Vacant
Sightless
Groping in primeval Night,
Needing God's advocates
To bring salvation to the prisoners
Without their civilizing mission
What fate awaits
Heart of Darkness!

Bell ringer

Pre-dawn,
When sleep is sweetest
He clangs me awake
To dubious duty of
Bartering responsibility with the unknown god
Metallic lunatic, you and your brother,
The muezzin
Vend faith at sundry times
In a sectarian god
That rips my soul asunder
Fridays and Sundays
Traffic of piety
Paralyze the land
Mantra-mouthers, roll up your sleeves
And fix our mess, else
Give me the Gods of the good life
Agnosticism, atheism or theism,
What does it matter?
Rid me of religion
And let there be prosperity, peace and security
And I shall have my beauty sleep.

Gospel according to Malala
(10 October, 2014)

Even though she walked
Through the SWAT valley
Of the shadow of the Taliban
Who could only shoot a body
But cannot shoot a dream,
Malala has sloughed off
Iron shawls of repression,
Gone to paradise and back,
Bearing celestial bouquets of Prometheus' fire
To light a dark world for children
Of all races, colours and creeds.
Avatar of Education for all
Malala has seized United Nations' podium
Borne her blazing torch to Buckingham
Streaked her meteor across Africa's skies
Shouting with the truly conscientious:
#BRING BACK OUR GIRLS!
A mere vessel of inchoate emotion
Chastened beyond her years
By grisly brew of Terror
Yet hooded goons of Negation
Quake behind their masks
At the sound of MALALA
Today as she ascends the Olympian heights
Of the Noble diadem
The whole world rises, her disciple.

Song of a rebel

Looku dem looku dem
Dem tink say dem wise
Who say? Una no wise
At all at all

Una say mek I no chop life:
Ciga na poison
"cigarret smokers are liable to die young".
But Oga dem dey smoke helele

Dem say for everywhere
Radio, TV, billboard
Even for church, mek I no
Wack woman.
Dem say she go give me STDs.
But everywhere I looku
I no know whether dese women
Naked or dem wear sometin;
Tight-tight cloth wey dey
Scatter man pickin head.

Drink nko?
Ah, dat one na gammalin 20!
"Give strong drink to him who is ready to perish"
Or how dem talk am sef?
Odeku, man pickin no go sip
Kaikai nko? For where?
Dem say mek I no drink at all at all
Dem say drinkers go go hell fire
Imagine!
How about beta chop;
Well-prepared wakis?
Dem say mek I no tink am.

Na gluttony be dat.

If beta gbedu dey play for radio
And I try to shake body
And do my waist
Laka dis, laka dat (2ce)
Hey, dem go vex plenty-plenty.
Na evil revelry be dat o.
You dey joke with hell fire, o,
Because you be Devil pickin.

If I work hard sef
And buy cars, private jets,
Sleep for 5-star hotel
And fly first class, go beach go sample
Fine-fine things for under the sunshine
Ah, na *baba nla* sin be dat!

Family go dey panic,
Friends go de hala
People go dey say:
"Live a good life and leave a good memory behind at death".

Memory my foot!
Na memory I go chop?
Wetin concern deadi body with memory?
All dis memory-memory sermon

Na *baba nla wuruwuru.*
Na *gibiti* people create am
Mek only dem chop life
Others go suffer until dem die.

Me, I don wise sef:
Give me all the sweet-sweet tings of life:
Give me wine, give me woman;
Give me beta chop;

Make I fly first class round the world;
Sing and dance;
And enjoy myself till I drop dead.
I ask you again:
Wetin concern deadi body with memory?

Ghost road

We left at midnight
Carrying only our backpacks
For on this journey of no return
Death was the only certainty:
From Abudu to Kano
We saw ghosts tilling their graveyards
Drinking their own blood for water
Here vultures are fat
Feasting on living offal
As we went, our weary ears
Were deafened with pious homilies of patriotism
All counselling stay-at-home
And die.
The toad loves water
But not when it is hot;
And if home is exile
Then let strangers keep my remains, I said.
These thoughts kept us company
From Kano through Niger
Libya and on the wastes of the Mediterranean
As we paddled and chugged our way
Across the watery grave at dead of night
Oh, between desert and the manicured lawns of Europe
Black bones littered the ocean floor
Dark urguries for the foolhard—
For on the sea to Italy
Or was it Spain or Malta?
What does it matter?
Our vessel as feared capsized
And we died by the thousands
Suddenly, it was Babel

No time for leavetaking
MA and BA certificates
Cherished keepsakes, photos of loved ones
And one or two goodluck amulets
All drowned with the body-bags.
We, the lucky survivors, awaited
Judgment Day in asylum gaol.
Yesterday as I left the Western Union money transfer counter
where I went to wire money home
It all came back to me.
Now I sit munching French fries and drinking black coffee
A European citizen.

SENTIMENTAL TRUTH

Moments
(For Elizabeth)

Again and Again
My sacrifice bears me
To your alcove, o great mountain.
Like a glowing ember
Placed by the gods upon a child's palm
A moment's delay spells grim scotching.
An enchanted devotee that I am
Following a ritual itinerary:
You stand poised in profile
O thou dream of loveliness
In finery of dew.
Drunk on your sights
More potent than the fiery draught
Of the palm
I glide from the marvelous curves
Of your sculpted hills of nectar
Affording a supple foothold
Toward your heavenly altitude.
And I journey, o goddess,
Through polished bliss of rounded sheers
Gaining in time the pair of honeyed domes
Aperch your dizzying scape
And, here, I strike camp
And rehearsed paradise beyond
The horizon, beyond.
Enraptured, I cling on as I glimpse heaven
Full of dreams
And as by magic, I find,
I am gliding in a fragrant sea.

Mother

I have come, Mother
And here are the items:
Salt, oil, water, kaoline,
White cloth —now
Let the dance begin
For the river today wears a treacherous smile

I have paddled a long distance
To meet you as always
Sharks and crocodiles waylaid my canoe
Seeking to capsize my craft
And devour your child, Mother!

Without your presence, Mother
I lean into void, clutch mirages for an anchor,
And stumble at high-noon for direction
It's a dark world, Mother
And love is alien here
They sow hate, cultivate selfishness
And transact life's trade with the cowries of ingratitude.

I have come, Mother
And here are the items:
Salt, oil, water, kaoline,
White cloth—now
Bless your child: give me, LOVE.

Woman

God's sparring partner
To whom men's blows
Are mere feints of preying-mantis
Goddess, all exert extremes of feats
To crack your smile
From field to table to bed
We struggle and strain
To win your flimsy festoon
That wilts with the setting sun
Witch and Angel
Saint and Seductress
Heaven and Hell
Like fire, you either incinerate
Or fashion-forth beauty spawn
Womb-man,
Woe-man
Woman
We men at your feet
Bow and worship.

Can't we love without making love?

My love, can't we love
Without making love?
See the nets that enmesh
Our feet: what do we tell
Pastor? How about our parents?
Even people will gossip
And the media will run riot
On our account.
Honey, can't we love without
Making love?
We kiss and caress
Fondle and fumble
External affairs
That do not provoke
Wars.
Darling, can't we love
Without making love?
Remember we both belong
To someone else
And you say that's the thrill
Sugar girl, can't we love
Without making love?

II

Sweetheart, can't we love
Without making love?
You say my eyes
Are newly-laid eggs of the dove
My lips, full and succulent,
Honeycombs of indescribable bliss
You tell me my breasts,

Full and erect,
Are African papaya
My flat belly resembles
A baby's *bombom*
And my buttocks
Are like the Okhuaghe hills
The nemesis of tired lorries.
But, honey pie can't we love
Without making love?

III

I kiss and caress you
Turning a blind eye
To your tobacco-stained teeth
And your *BO* that kills
All cologne on arrival
You say my body's a tourist haunt
And you want to explore
My inner landscapes.
Dearie, can't we just love,
Yes, love
Without making love?

IV

Can't we love
without making love?
AIDS IS REAL!!!
And so are other STDs!
How about an unwanted pregnancy;
And myriad hazards of copulation?
Honey, can't we love
Without making love?

Heart cry

Marooned in the far end
Of the world
The Sahara and the Atlantic
Stand between you and me, but
Your voice, potent and eager, floats
Into my longing ear
From the cellphone
Which brings news of home and our
Shared moments revisited
A traveller far away from home
I yearn for your laughing eyes and inviting lips
I reach out in vain for your bulbous boobs
And grope absent-mindedly for your downy valley
Where you and I romp like passionate gazelles
In lonely niches
My Angel of the morning, joy of my soul, this
Distance makes our love fonder, intoxicating like strong drink
As I see lovers kissing in crowded boulevards here
And I suffer culture shock
For their sincere expression of affection
That stabs my prude heart
Oh, the seconds lumber to minutes and
Minutes labour in the delivery room of tardy hours
That trundle to lengthening days
That fill me with fever of longing
Each dawning day brings us closer
Shrinking time, bridging distance
For soon we shall be lost
In our famished embrace.

I love

I love heaven on earth:
The laughter of children
The heady fragrance of lovers
The well-wrought music
And the art/act of conversation
I love heaven:
The well-chiselled figured woman
Ample-proportioned, generous hips and bouncing bosom
And her laughter the sound of happy cymbals
I love competition:
Breasting the tape before the chasing pack
Fired by the spirit of excellence
To make the world a better place.
I love life:
The beautiful game
Football
And, yes, I love ... Literature

Lead us not into temptation

Lead us not into temptation
For we shall find it ourselves
In watering-holes in patched pathways
In netared hives that colonize
Our roving fantasia,
In rivers of honey which flow in the crook
Between purgatory and hell
Until we enter through the labia-gates
Into paradise to shame the Devil and his ponces
Who coat sundry baits
With sweetmeats that clog the throat
To provoke terminal hemorrhage
But we're wise to their gambits
The fish we shall take, the bone shun.

Ètù for life

(For Muyiwa)

What is this! What is this!! What is this!!!
Ètùmàlè!!!
Twin calabashes clashing, clashing,
Rolling, riveting, holding your eyes captive:
They set your soul on fire
As sweet flames of animal desire
Loosen your eager loins;
Your expectant palate parched drools and the heart beats
Kati-Kati Kati-Kati as
Etu dances fire dance, the erotic rhythm
The liquid gait of a practised seductress
Oyayi!!!
Ètùmàlè! You are my Helen
Come set my Troy on fire;
You are my Queen Sheba
Ravage my fabled kingdom
You are my African Queen
My Brazil! My America!!
From Arse-hole Rock to Sambisa
From Cape to Cairo
You drive us all to cusps of dreams
Engine of growth, leaven of nascent doughs
All hail: Ètù for life.

Privacy

We now keep our trysts
In the marketplace
The invites having been sent
Way ahead of the voyeurs' feast.
Love, can you hear the crowd?
Is that cheering or jeering?
How can you say you can't decipher?
Do you not send your wigs to *eBay*;
Your brassiere to *Facebook*;
And your panties to *Instagram*?
Now, love, our secret thing
Is primetime stuff
Entertaining the pleasure-mad crowd
Denying us, you and I, even a fig-leaf
To screen our shame.

Now, tell me, Love, is our affair now
A penny piece of scandal
To slake the lurid hunger
Of a prudish world?
Is this what gives you the thrill:
Is ours now a mini-Big Brother show?
Is Orwell's *1984* now our grundnorm?
But remember when this show
Will have run its fevered course,
Our audience will forever hoard
Our shame in their devices.

Marriage, love and sex

Jane's was the stuff
Of legend, for her affair
With John Thomas scoffed at
Common yarn spinners
Who drenched other loves in the village spittoon
Along the river routes or the kneaded farm-path
Under the spreading Almond
At the village square or trysting corners
Jane and John made reckless love
Such that the neighbourhood Billy
Went coy and the stray Bingo drooled with envy
Scandalized custom made the lovebirds
Its favourite present: the nuptials
That hushed the loquacious market to the day
Few market-days hence
Jane's fireside went cold
John Thomas, limp and flaccid,
Fanned the reluctant embers to numb ash:
For love had made a run for it
Shortly after the last guests had departed.

The other woman

Wife, quack the wronged mother hen
And deafen the 'hood's censorious ears
All you please but remember those long lonely nights
On sundering mat, when
Speech lost her tongue between you and me
And your food tasted an ill-prepared burnt-offering
For a niggardly god
She it was who held the fort
Massaging my bruised ego
Feeding my ulcerous maw and,
What's more, warming those icy nights
With her fulsome bounties, giving
And giving life's little extras
That lighten the road's tedium
Sweeten the workaday drudgeries I'm condemned to do
For you and the brood
And laying all her store
At my feet as though
I were the latest minted deity
Entitled to a woman's honeyed orifices.
True, they call her names
Which wrong her hallowed calling
Even the book rebukes her toilings
To help maintain my sanity
Yet hers is the unsung caregiver
Deserving the un-common diadem
For like all the shadowy givers
We should chant her paean in the marketplace.

Ucheka

We'd hoped for a little queen
To Mama's cloistered realm
A joy bundle for weekends' preening sessions:
Colourful ribbons and sundry bling-blings for her adornment
To charm the living room at visiting times
And picnicking gambols.
But the gods disposed, trumping mortals' caprices.
There you are, pure joy dispenser
Innocence's chief ambassador
Streaking light amid stumps of darkness and surfeited drear;
Lisping human tongue in chirpings of sweetness
In your nacent darings
Future feats of brawn and brain
Make themselves bare
Even to the cynical crowd, the mixed multitudes of killjoy.
Go, then, powered by parents' orisons
Into a world waiting for your distillates
Of great annunciation
Reign and rule over all that moves, friends and foes, alike
Great and small, all matter salaaming
Let the four winds hear and obey your voice always
Sun and moon, stars and all Nature
Anticipate your every need and meet it
As joy, son, fills the earth
Rejoicing the living, the undead and the unborn.

Kill me

Kill me
Not with bombs and bullets
Boulders and bludgeons
Stones and sticks
Kill me
Beloved
With showers of honey
The dizzying Nirvana
Of your succulence
Kill me
With surfeits of romance
The steamy wrestle, the painful pleasures
Of orgiastics, the *uuhs* and *aahs*
Of mutual passion
Kill me,
Oh, kill me quick
With the juicy orifices of your nectar
Up and down
Back and front
Loaded, padded, miracle of curves
Eagle-down, magic carpet gliding
To paradise
Ah, Baby
Kill meeee
With love.

Song of the mating flies

Look away, o man, from our
Rendezvous, Lovey and I
Anus to anus interlocked
Askance at a prudish world

See our canine brethren doing
Their thing, anus to anus glued
Oblivious to sanctimonious
Onlookers

Then consider Mister Cockerel
Restless, always in hot pursuit
Of Lady Hen,
Tired of coquetry, she stoops
To conquer the Alpha plumage

Billy and Nanny, they
Deafen the neighbourhood ears with eager bleats
For Billy, his rotund mother's
Prima Donna,
The crowning prize of a hard day's work.

Let Lovey and I be, then
Prurient judges of morality
And let us keep our tryst
As our bent dictates.

Morountodun

(For Sarah)

My
Feet
Parched

     and
          calloused
With myriad journeys
Searching for you:
The Lone fulcrum of my essence.

        Yet
In this strip of Hell's
Temporal outpost
You spread your bounties
Like a gushing spring
Before a famished sojourner ...

You have given me life
Yes, life has been born,
     Anew
Like the laughters of flowers ...

I am the lobe of a kola nut
And you, my other half.
Shall these two lobes cleave
A whole to form?
I wait:
WILL YOU YIELD?

11/12/1995

HOME TRUTH

For Chinelo

All's quiet now ...
The breathless climb to the sixth floor,
The burnt-out energy; the confused maze
Of clashing lecture hours;
The stress that accompanies you to the lecturer's
Office to beat the deadline ...
All's quiet now ...

Time's running out:
Exams are around the corner,
Turn in your project by—or else,
Extra year!

The Department does not understand;
And now, my love—they all get in the way.
I take the pounding like Balaam's Ass.
All's quiet now ...

Indeed, all earth's treasures are but dross:
The fabled Golden Fleece, the itch of desire,
The noisy pride of achievement and the
Sundry ceremonies of fools.
Tis all dust to dust. Silence ...
Rest, Chinelo, for all's quiet now.

Fate

Was it my fault
That I was born in Gaza,
A crime punishable by Genocide
That I genuflect to a different god;
Shia or Sunni, what does it matter
If I chant "Die Not, Except As A Muslim"?
Yet, ISIS is not amused
The Gulf is gulfed, splintered into shards
Of a kaleidoscopic God ...
Look West, the rain
The rain of acid in Ukraine
MH 17 *buk*-ed, no story
The lethal argument continues ...
Then, look East, the Taliban,
The Taliban have banned compassion
In Afghanistan, Pakistan, Waziristan
And all the *stans* there are ...
Oh, is it my fault, indeed,
That I was born at the epicentre
Of the Hurricane, Tornado, Volcano
Flash-floods, Earthquakes!
Is it my fault?
Is it, Oh Lord, my fault?
That I took root in the eye of the storm;
In a neighbourhood of Boko Haram?
And, now, of EBOLA?
Lord, is it my fault?

Remembering to forget

Gather our children away
From History which dogs like an implacable
Avenger, a witness to the metamorphoses of love:
Muslim father drunk on the aphrodisiac of rebellion
Took a kaffir maid to the altar
And the gods gave their blessing with
A school of innocents
Oblivious to the clashes of civilizations
Raging in far away lands
Yet rocking, rocking home and hearth

Contrary beliefs are a sleeping volcano
That covers the town in ash of extinction
Without a moment's notice:
Father butchers mother before children
And buries the infidel wife in a shallow grave

That was then, this is now:
History haunts and hunts our children
Whose memories sear like fire
Licking the hay of happiness
And peace lies in pieces
In their remembering minds

Truth is a village lunatic hawking public shame
And private indiscretions in the marketplace
Buyers flee from his shocking wares like the plague
And yet truth follows them wherever they go

Gather, then, our children away
From History, from truth that defies their humanity
And let them remember to forget.

The rich destitute

He stands
Daily by the roadside
Bowl in hand, and
At times in far countries,
World capitals and icy nooks
Scavenging dumpsites of the blessed.
He is a rich king of the earth
Of that, there's no doubt
He basks in the eternal sunshine
And the rain falls always in due season
His soil teems with a thousand diamonds
And oceans of crude lie in the womb of the earth,
His earth.
Envy of the world
Sleeping Giant
Creepers and rodents play hide-and-seek on his drowsy face
Even as strangers take turn to rape him
Leaving him, useless ...

His palace is the world's toilet,
His land choked with castoffs
From toothpick to tractor
He has no say in the matter
Else he shall go to bed, hungry ...

He has eyes but leans on others to show the way;
His ears are but fancy lobes, the butt of alien comedians
The contents of his skull are the stuff of soothsayers
Eternal toddler, grey and grizzled at noon
The world keeps him at a safe distance
To remind it of its Genesis.

The iroko has fallen

(For my late uncle, Chief Felix Okoh)

The Iroko has fallen
Suddenly the forest undergrowth
Bears the balded head of *gorimapa*
As the shade provided by the Iroko is gone
With the fallen giant.
The Iroko has fallen
Suddenly the forest is a desert
Crops and creepers weep their loss
Rodents and reptiles stake a claim
To chunks of the supine behemoth
The Iroko has fallen
Suddenly the community is naked
Verigo dazes hoary heads
And the young are lost for words
As all wonder who will shield the clan
From reprobate gales?
The Iroko has fallen
Ah, the forest giant has crashed to the earth
The forest searches for a loincloth
To cover her rude shame
The Iroko, the Iroko has f-a-l-l-e-n ...

Death

(For Felix Okoh)

It is not the crash of the Iroko that matters
It is the silence afterwards
The deafening silence in which you ask:
God, where's your sense of proportion?
Do you've to kill a fly with a boulder?
Where's your sense of justice?
Suddenly you are overcome with a sense of cluelessness
Like a baby in the wilderness
Without the benefit of GPS?
You're left with a sense of helplessness.
The insecurity called Life
Finally comes home
And sits beside you.

Death is a fallacy

(For Chigbo Ekwealo)

Armed with a sole philosopher's stone,
You took life-long aim at Death:
A restless David high on knowledge-hubris
On the treacherous crag littered with the blanched remains
Of fore-seekers, you jabbed, feinted, ducked in time
To parry a wayward roundhouse,
Your opponent, a veteran unknown to have conceded
A bout to mortals—
Yet, you preserved.
In your hunter's pouch, time-tested argumentums:
Rugged Reason hoisted on Inductions and Deductions
Your claims always valid and your premises sound;
But the one fallacy that felled Plato,
Torpedoed Aristotle and killed Kant and company
Has alas proved your terminal rebuttal.
Yet the living must look beyond this deluge of tears
That overcasts the Akoka skies
for a rendezvous with truth:
Death's a pin-prick that deflates man's vaulting airs
In hours of glory.
Envy not, Death's latest conquest
For whom the Truth now stands revealed.
Perched on the other side of the flesh
No more, for him, the treacheries of fast-friends
No more, the peskiness of APER-drunk colleagues
Forever haggling over rickety chairs;
No more for the traveller the dull jingles of beggars' coins.
All, all the certification of earth's dross is now on ICE.
Tomorrow, the earth will have its dinner,
Awaiting its next breakfast-you or me.

Love in the time of Ebola
(In memory of *Chigbo Ekwealo)

Baami returned from work much earlier
Than usual, retching, eyes rheumy with fire
From hell and vomiting offensive sandwich
And like mother hen, *Maami* gathered us,
Five pillars of the line, under her wings
Safe, safe, far from our dying dad.
It's standard medical procedure, we were told:
For, love is suicide in the season of plagues
That visit the community like predatory hawks.
He managed his longsuffering beetle
Snaking and roaching his way to hospital
Groggily he staggered to doctor's door
Scapel flying and heavenly robe billowing
The specialist led the 100 metre dash for the exit door
Patients and personnel alike
Fled the sanctuary as *Baami* found himself
In a desert full of echoes
Later, much later, the expert returned, a crowd in tow, his
Gloved hands probed the patient for signs
And he declared: 'He couldn't make it; move *it* to the morgue'.

---

*   *Dr Chigbo Joseph Ekwealo of Philosophy Department, UNILAG
    died on 7 September, 2014; he was reportedly shunned for hours
    by doctors on duty at the Adi-Araba Hospital in the mistaken
    belief that he was an Ebola patient until he died in the ambulance
    that had conveyed him from the Unilag Medical Centre.*

For whom is it well?

Battered and bruised and broken
Chasing shadows which belie life's true emptinesses
Womb wish offers a respite
But Mother sings her fond cautionary tale:
For whom is it well?
The world is full of poor people
Who daily labour to be rich
Yet in their poverty they find happiness.
But not comfort;
The rich play god over men
As though they created fulfillment
The world's greatest treasures they amass
Yet they have houses, not a home
To duck from sorrow
Look at our rulers, they hold the power of life and death,
Or so it seems.
Ruin and call it rulership
Destroy and label it Development
Endless run of locusts
Waging war against the forest to gain green happiness
But drought drains their body-poliic
Lack has it uses, son ...
I look around, then, and see
Wisdom's proof: rich and poor
All need levels on groveling ground
Searching for happiness the gods alone dispense
To whomsoever favour follows.
*A'a rhigu mma ...
Aá rhigu mma ...

---

* *For whom is it well? in Ika dialect*

Be prepared

[Song: There's a whole lot of people going home ...]

Tony left the other day
Right in the middle of fun
Suzie too in the lap of fortune
And grizzled grandies still stick around
Taking all with philosophical calmness

There's a whole lot of people going home ...

You look at last year's photo
The smile freezes on your face
As you recognize the steady depletion:
Love, standing by your side
All picture of beauty and rude health
Is gone, without a goodbye;
To your near left, Bob
The ladies' man, the Black Adonis
Himself, left in mangled metal
On the road, the doctors pronounced him *BID** and
If you listen closely
You will hear dying snivellings of mourners ...

There's a whole lot of people going home ...

Death's no respecter of status, class or connections
The leveller who brings princes and paupers
To dust; he prowls the road, cudgel in hand,
Clubbing wayfarers to death.
But you go about your business,
Fancy-free
Secure in your armour
Of self-righteousness

And, somehow you feel:
Others may, I cannot.
Yet a voice whispers
Be prepared ...

There's a lot of people going home ...

---

* *BID: Brought In Dead*

I Believe

I believe
I believe in love:
Self-giving to the other in the total absence of praise-singers
And no expectations to self; a self-emptying which enriches
the other,
Blood, friend or foe
All have a share of my heart.

I believe
I believe in the universal brotherhood of man,
The incredible human capacity to scale all hurdles
In life's sinuous path, in the god, and not the dog
In man.

I believe
I believe in woman: mother, sister, cousin, niece, friend,
Yes, a woman-friend who contains multitudes
Happily bringing gifts and sacrifices to my undeserving altar.
I believe, oh
I believe in a child
The glory of innocence
Paradise incarnate, glimpsed in laughter and beauty
The little god; he, then, who violates it, betrays God
And commits the worst crime.
Worship therefore at its feet and gain peace.

I believe
I believe in the nationhood of all peoples
Colour-blind and Babel-rejecting. For
If our forebears ventured to poke heaven in the face
Why not us? Let us therefore dream, dare, *believe*.

I believe

I believe in God: Master-designer, Primal Architect, the
Creator,
The Cause. Nature's His first evangelist
Let's follow Nature, God's being, to His presence
Let everything that has breath praise God
I believe
I believe in laughter
Freedom from law, forged in fear
To hush laughter's celebrations
Live and let live's the golden rule
Don't break it
For all who the law keep
Enter heaven and the law breaker
Partakes of hell-all on earth domiciled.

I believe
Yes, I believe in the equality of all men
There are no slaves, no princes born
Raze down the slums of deprivation
Wherever they may be found
Demolish all palaces of privilege
And let's build equal dwellings for all.

Kraftgriots

Also in the series (POETRY) *continued*

Ebi Yeibo: *Maiden Lines* (2004)
Barine Ngaage: *Rhythms of Crisis* (2004)
Funso Aiyejina: *I,The Supreme & Other Poems* (2004)
'Lere Oladitan: *Boolekaja: Lagos Poems 1* (2005)
Seyi Adigun: *Bard on the Shore* (2005)
Famous Dakolo: *A Letter to Flora* (2005)
Olawale Durojaiye: *An African Night* (2005)
G. 'Ebinyo Ogbowei: *let the honey run & other poems* (2005)
Joe Ushie: *Popular Stand & Other Poems* (2005)
Gbemisola Adeoti: *Naked Soles* (2005)
Aj. Dagga Tolar: *This Country is not a Poem* (2005)
Tunde Adeniran: *Labyrinthine Ways* (2006)
Sophia Obi: *Tears in a Basket* (2006)
Tonyo Biriabebe: *Undercurrents* (2006)
Ademola O. Dasylva: *Songs of Odamolugbe* (2006), winner, 2006 ANA/Cadbury
     poetry prize
George Ehusani: *Flames of Truth* (2006)
Abubakar Gimba: *This Land of Ours* (2006)
G. 'Ebinyo Ogbowei: *the heedless ballot box* (2006)
Hyginus Ekwuazi: *Love Apart* (2006), winner, 2007 ANA/NDDC Gabriel Okara
     poetry prize and winner, 2007 ANA/Cadbury poetry prize
Abubakar Gimba: *Inner Rumblings* (2006)
Albert Otto: *Letters from the Earth* (2007)
Aj. Dagga Tolar: *Darkwaters Drunkard* (2007)
Idris Okpanachi: *The Eaters of the Living* (2007), winner, 2008 ANA/Cadbury
     poetry prize
Tubal-Cain: *Mystery in Our Stream* (2007), winner, 2006 ANA/NDDC Gabriel
     Okara poetry prize
John Iwuh: *Ashes & Daydreams* (2007)
Sola Owonibi: *Chants to the Ancestors* (2007)
Adewale Aderinale: *The Authentic* (2007)
Ebi Yeibo: *The Forbidden Tongue* (2007)
Doutimi Kpakiama: *Salute to our Mangrove Giants* (2008)
Halima M. Usman: *Spellbound* (2008)
Hyginus Ekwuazi: *Dawn Into Moonlight: All Around Me Dawning* (2008), winner,
     2008 ANA/NDDC Gabriel Okara poetry prize
Ismail Bala Garba & Abdullahi Ismaila (eds.): *Pyramids: An Anthology of Poems
     from Northern Nigeria* (2008)
Denja Abdullahi: *Abuja Nunyi (This is Abuja)* (2008)
Japhet Adeneye: *Poems for Teenagers* (2008)
Seyi Hodonu: *A Tale of Two in Time (Letters to Susan)* (2008)
Ibukun Babarinde: *Running Splash of Rust and Gold* (2008)
Chris Ngozi Nkoro: *Trails of a Distance* (2008)
Tunde Adeniran: *Beyond Finalities* (2008)

Abba Abdulkareem: *A Bard's Balderdash* (2008)
Ifeanyi D. Ogbonnaya: *... And Pigs Shall Become House Cleaners* (2008)
Ebinyo Ogbowei: *the town crier's song* (2009)
Ebinyo Ogbowei: *song of a dying river* (2009)
Sophia Obi-Apoko: *Floating Snags* (2009)
Akachi Adimora-Ezeigbo: *Heart Songs* (2009), winner, 2009 ANA/Cadbury poetry prize
Hyginus Ekwuazi: *The Monkey's Eyes* (2009)
Seyi Adigun: *Prayer for the Mwalimu* (2009)
Faith A. Brown: *Endless Season* (2009)
B.M. Dzukogi: *Midnight Lamp* (2009)
B.M. Dzukogi: *These Last Tears* (2009)
Chimezie Ezechukwu: *The Nightingale* (2009)
Ummi Kaltume Abdullahi: *Tiny Fingers* (2009)
Ismaila Bala & Ahmed Maiwada (eds.): *Fireflies: An Anthology of New Nigerian Poetry* (2009)
Eugenia Abu: *Don't Look at Me Like That* (2009)
Data Osa Don-Pedro: *You Are Gold and Other Poems* (2009)
Sam Omatseye: *Mandela's Bones and Other Poems* (2009)
Sam Omatseye: *Dear Baby Ramatu* (2009)
C.O. Iyimoga: *Fragments in the Air* (2010)
Bose Ayeni-Tsevende: *Streams* (2010)
Seyi Hodonu: *Songs from My Mother's Heart (2010)*, winner ANA/NDDC Gabriel Okara poetry prize, 2010
Akachi Adimora-Ezeigbo: *Waiting for Dawn* (2010)
Hyginus Ekwuazi: *That Other Country* (2010), winner, ANA/Cadbury poetry prize, 2010
Emmanuel Frank-Opigo: *Masks and Facades* (2010)
Tosin Otitoju: *Comrade* (2010)
Arnold Udoka: *Poems Across Borders* (2010)
Arnold Udoka: *The Gods Are So Silent & Other Poems* (2010)
Abubakar Othman: *The Passions of Cupid* (2010)
Okinba Launko: *Dream-Seeker on Divining Chain* (2010)
'kufre ekanem: *the ant eaters* (2010)
McNezer Fasehun: *Ever Had a Dear Sister* (2010)
Baba S. Umar: *A Portrait of My People* (2010)
Gimba Kakanda: *Safari Pants* (2010)
Sam Omatseye: *Lion Wind & Other Poems* (2011)
Ify Omalicha: *Now that Dreams are Born* (2011)
Karo Okokoh: *Souls of a Troubadour* (2011)
Ada Onyebuenyi, Chris Ngozi Nkoro, Ebere Chukwu (eds): *Uto Nka: An Anthology of Literature for Fresh Voices* (2011)
Mabel Osakwe: *Desert Songs of Bloom* (2011)
Pious Okoro: *Vultures of Fortune & Other Poems* (2011)
Godwin Yina: *Clouds of Sorrows* (2011)
Nnimmo Bassey: *I Will Not Dance to Your Beat* (2011)
Denja Abdullahi: *A Thousand Years of Thirst* (2011)
Enoch Ojotisa: *Commoner's Speech* (2011)
Rowland Timi Kpakiama: *Bees and Beetles* (2011)
Niyi Osundare: *Random Blues* (2011)

Lawrence Ogbo Ugwuanyi: *Let Them Not Run* (2011)
Saddiq M. Dzukogi: *Canvas* (2011
Arnold Udoka: *Running with My Rivers* (2011)
Olusanya Bamidele: *Erased Without a Trace* (2011)
Olufolake Jegede: *Treasure Pods* (2012)
Karo Okokoh: *Songs of a Griot* (2012), winner. ANA/NDDC Gabriel Okara
    poetry prize, 2012
Musa Idris Okpanachi: *From the Margins of Paradise* (2012)
John Martins Agba: *The Fiend and Other Poems* (2012)
Sunnie Ododo: *Broken Pitchers* (2012)
'Kunmi Adeoti: *Epileptic City* (2012)
Ibiwari Ikiriko: *Oily Tears of the Delta* (2012)
Bala Dalhatu: *Moonlights* (2012)
Karo Okokoh: *Manna for the Mind* (2012)
Chika O. Agbo: *The Fury of the Gods* (2012)
Emmanuel C. S. Ojukwu: *Beneath the Sagging Roof* (2012)
Amirikpa Oyigbenu: *Cascades and Flakes* (2012)
Ebi Yeibo: *Shadows of the Setting Sun* (2012)
Chikaoha Agoha: *Shreds of Thunder* (2012)
Mark Okorie: *Terror Verses* (2012)
Clemmy Igwebike-Ossi: *Daisies in the Desert* (2012)
Idris Amali: *Back Again (At the Foothills of Greed)* (2012)
A.N. Akwanya: *Visitant on Tiptoe* (2012)
Akachi Adimora-Ezeigbo: *Dancing Masks* (2013)
Chinazo-Bertrand Okeomah: *Furnace of Passion* (2013)
g'ebinyŏ ogbowei: *marsh boy and other poems* (2013)
Ifeoma Chinwuba: *African Romance* (2013)
Remi Raji: *Sea of my Mind* (2013)
Francis Odinya: *Never Cry Again in Babylon* (2013)
Immanuel Unekwuojo Ogu: *Musings of a Pilgrim* (2013)
Khabyr Fasasi: *Tongues of Warning* (2013)
J.C.P. Christopher: *Salient Whispers* (2014)
Paul T. Liam: *Saint Sha'ade and other poems* (2014)
Joy Nwiyi: *Burning Bottom* (2014)
R. Adebayo Lawal: *Melodreams* (2014)
R. Adebayo Lawal: *Music of the Muezzin* (2014)
Idris Amali: *Efeega: War of Ants* (2014)
Samuel Onungwe: *Tantrums of a King* (2014)
Bizuum G. Yadok: *Echoes of the Plateau* (2014)
Abubakar Othman: *Bloodstreams in the Desert* (2014)
rome aboh: *A torrent of terror* (2014)
Fodio Ahmed: *Thirst* (2015)
Udenta O. Udenta: *37 Seasons Before the Tornado* (2015)
Magnus Abraham-Dukuma: *Dreams from the Creeks* (2015)
Christian Otobotekere: *The Sailor's Son 1* (2015)
Tanure Ojaide: *The Tale of the Harmattan* (2015)
Festus Okwekwe: *Our Mother Is Not A Woman* (2015)
Khabyr Fasasi: *Spells of Solemn Songs* (2015)
Tunde Adeniran: *Fate and Faith* (2015)

Printed in the United States
By Bookmasters